# Faraway Worlds

*Planets Beyond
Our Solar System*

*Paul Halpern*

*Illustrated by Lynette R. Cook*

Charlesbridge

To Aden, Eli, and Felicia, for their love and support — P. H.

To my parents and the generations before, from whom I have received my artistic talent,
my love of science, and a legacy of exploration — L. R. C.

The author and illustrator gratefully acknowledge Alyssa Mito Pusey for her editorial work
and Sarah McAbee for her design assistance. Charlesbridge would like to thank Dr. Irene Porro,
Education and Public Outreach Scientist at the MIT Center for Space Research, and
Dr. Geoff Marcy, Professor of Astronomy at the University of California, Berkeley.

The paintings in this book are based on recent astronomical discoveries.
The illustrator has filled in the details using her knowledge of science
and her artistic license as an astronomical illustrator.

Text copyright © 2004 by Paul Halpern
Illustrations copyright © 2004 by Lynette R. Cook
All rights reserved, including the right of reproduction in whole
    or in part in any form. Charlesbridge and colophon are registered
    trademarks of Charlesbridge Publishing, Inc.
Published by Charlesbridge, 85 Main Street, Watertown, MA 02472
(617) 926-0329 • www.charlesbridge.com

Library of Congress Cataloging-in-Publication Data
Halpern, Paul, 1961-
    Faraway worlds : planets beyond our solar system / Paul Halpern ;
illustrated by Lynette Cook.
        p. cm.
Includes index.
Summary: An introduction to the search for and discovery of planets
outside our solar system and what life may be like on such distant
worlds.
    ISBN 1-57091-616-0 (reinforced for library use)
    ISBN 1-57091-617-9 (softcover)
1. Planets—Juvenile literature. [1. Planets.]   I. Cook, Lynette, ill.
II. Title.
QB602.H35 2004
523.2'4—dc22        2003021570

Printed in China
    (hc)    10 9 8 7 6 5 4 3 2 1
    (sc)    10 9 8 7 6 5 4 3 2 1

Imagine a world far beyond our solar system.

A place full of deadly gases, heated to a scalding 2,000 degrees.

A planet where a year is only three and a half days long.

Could such a place really exist?

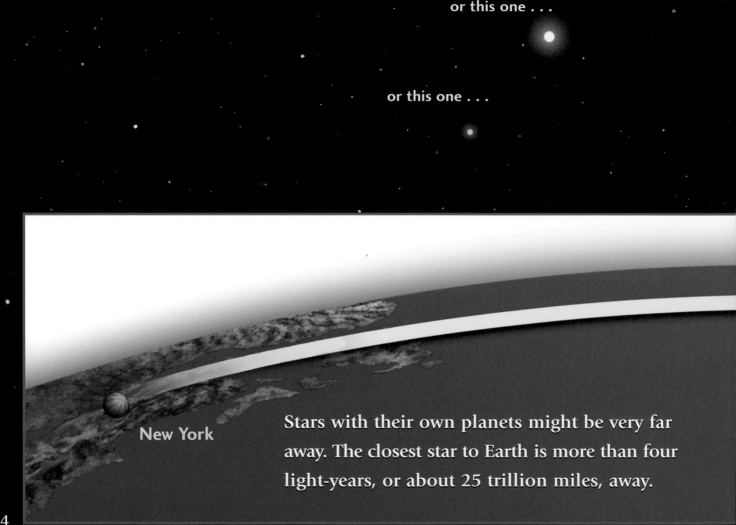

or this one . . .

or this one . . .

New York

Stars with their own planets might be very far
away. The closest star to Earth is more than four
light-years, or about 25 trillion miles, away.

4

The prefix *extra-* means *beyond*. Something that is *extraordinary* is beyond the ordinary, or unusual. An *extraterrestrial* alien is from beyond Earth, or from outer space. An *extrasolar* planet is beyond our solar system. An extraterrestrial from an extrasolar planet would be extraordinary!

Earth

Sun

Finding extrasolar planets is not easy. Planets are small compared to stars. If our Sun were the size of a basketball, the Earth would be a tiny pea.

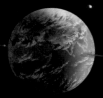

If you stood in New York and held a basketball to represent our Sun, a basketball representing the closest star would be in Germany.

Germany

Planet hunters face yet another challenge: unlike stars, planets do not shine with their own visible light. Planets are more like bicycle reflectors, which can be seen only when light bounces off them.

A planet's reflected light is dim compared to the light of a shining star. Even with a powerful telescope, it would be almost impossible to see the tiny glow of an extrasolar planet amid the dazzling brightness of its sun.

Most of the telescopes used today are optical telescopes. An optical telescope gathers light in the same way that a funnel gathers water. It collects and concentrates faint light so that the human eye can see it better.

We can look through an optical telescope and see the other planets in our solar system. We can even see far-off galaxies. But we cannot see extrasolar planets, because they are too distant and they do not reflect enough light.

Imagine standing in the dark, miles away from a huge campfire, trying to spot a single marshmallow toasting over the fire. Even with binoculars, such a feat would be nearly impossible.

If extrasolar planets are so hard to see, how do astronomers hunt for them? They track down clues. A good clue is a star that wobbles.

Stars and planets attract each other by gravity. The gravitational force of a star holds its planets in orbit. But the planets also pull back on the star, causing it to wobble a little.

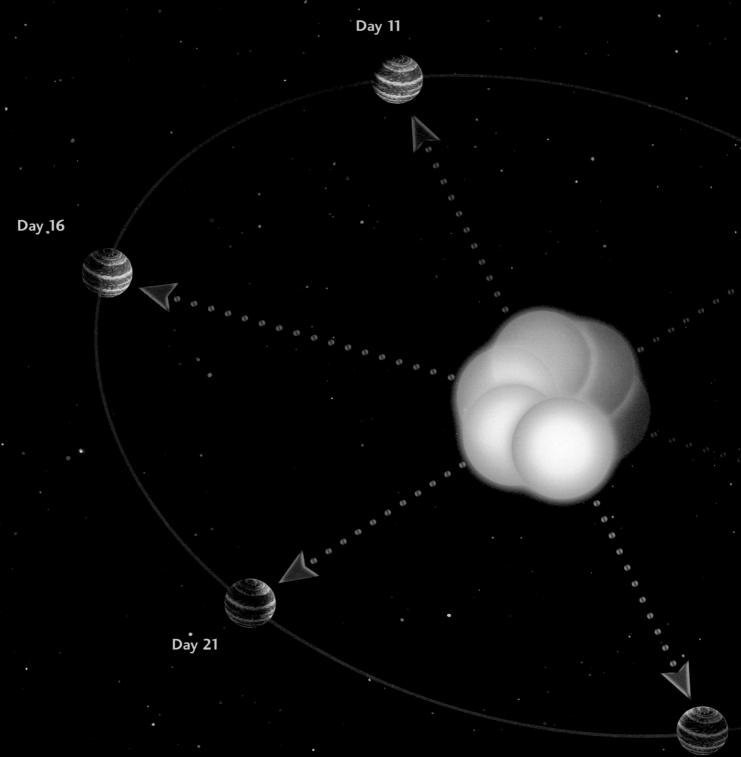

Day 11

Day 16

Day 21

Day 26

To picture a wobbling star, imagine a girl named Stella walking her dogs at dusk. Stella's small, black dogs are difficult to see in the near-darkness. On the other hand, Stella is easily visible in her bright clothes and light-up running shoes. Even when you cannot see the dogs, you can see Stella.

How do you know that Stella is walking her dogs and not just walking alone? Every time a dog pulls on its leash, Stella lurches in its direction. Again and again, her dogs pull her, causing her to wobble as she walks.

**Day 6**

Like Stella, a star can wobble, showing that it is being pulled by something. This invisible something could be a planet.

**Day 1**

This planet orbits its star every 30 days. As the planet circles the star, it pulls the star in different directions, causing the star to wobble.

If the light seems bluer than normal, then the star is moving toward us.

If the light looks redder, then the star is moving away from us.
This is called the Doppler effect.

These color shifts are so tiny that they cannot be seen with
the unaided eye, but planet hunters can measure them with
special telescopes.

You can experience the Doppler effect right here on Earth.
The Doppler effect applies to sound as well as light.
A rising pitch means that an object is moving toward
the listener. A falling pitch means that it is moving away.

Higher pitch

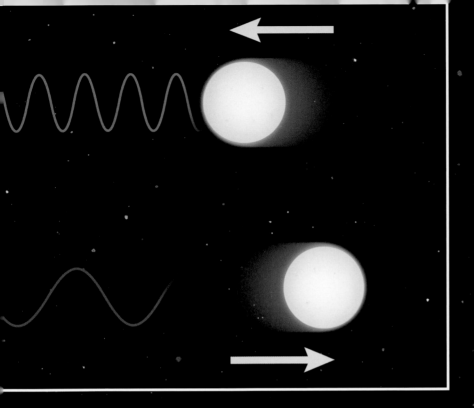

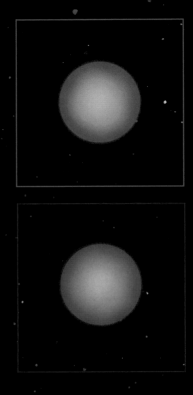

If a star appears redder, then bluer, then redder, then bluer, over and over again, then it is wobbling. It is slightly closer, then slightly farther away, then closer, then farther away again.

Listen carefully the next time a fire engine races by with its siren blaring. As the fire engine comes closer to you, its siren sounds higher and higher. But as the fire engine goes away, its siren sounds lower and lower. This is an example of the Doppler effect.

Lower pitch

11

In 1995, a group of Swiss astronomers led by Michel Mayor (mee-SHELL my-YOR) and Didier Queloz (DEE-dee-yay kay-LO) focused their telescope on a star named 51 Pegasi (PEG-ah-see). This star is more than a hundred trillion miles from Earth in the constellation known as the Great Square of Pegasus. To the astronomers, 51 Pegasi seemed a little bluer, then a little redder, then bluer, then redder.

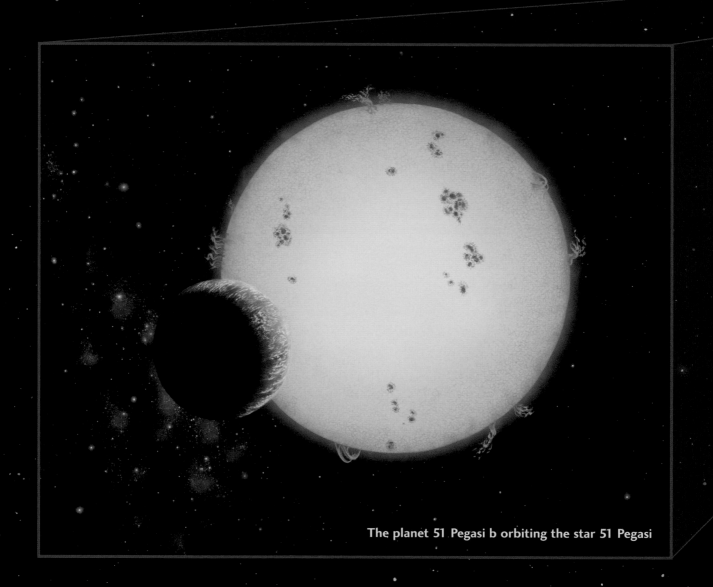

The planet 51 Pegasi b orbiting the star 51 Pegasi

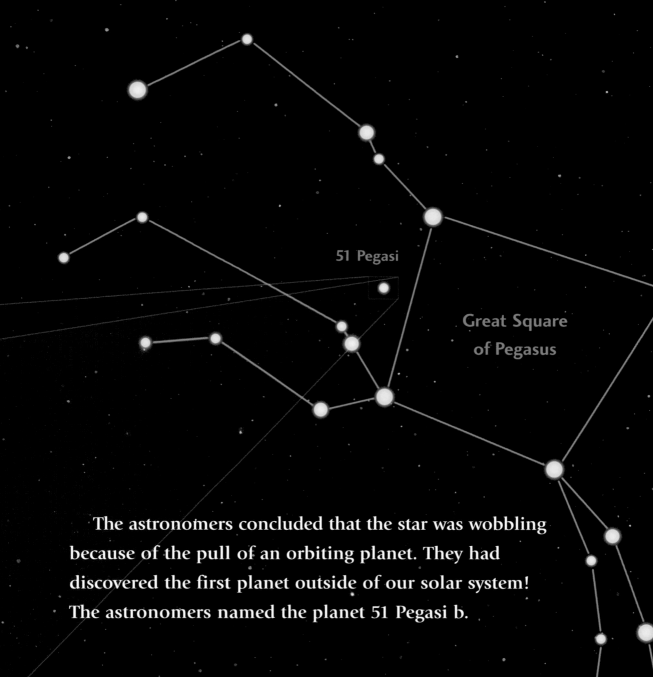

51 Pegasi

Great Square
of Pegasus

The astronomers concluded that the star was wobbling because of the pull of an orbiting planet. They had discovered the first planet outside of our solar system! The astronomers named the planet 51 Pegasi b.

51 Pegasi b is the first known planet orbiting a shining star similar to our Sun. However, other planets beyond the solar system were discovered before it. In 1992, the Polish astronomer Alex Wolszczan (WOLSH-chen) found new planets orbiting around a pulsar, the rapidly spinning core of a dead star.

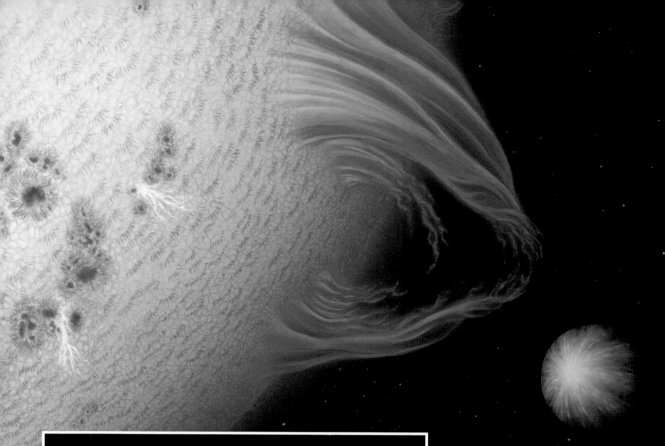

A planet orbiting a red binary (twin) star, as seen from a nearby asteroid

The planet Upsilon Andromedae b and its star

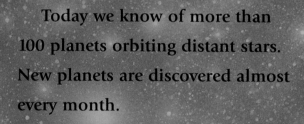

Today we know of more than 100 planets orbiting distant stars. New planets are discovered almost every month.

Are these newfound planets similar to Earth? Could humans live on these worlds someday? Would we meet alien creatures there?

The planet HD 46375 b, with a ring particle shown up close

The unconfirmed Lalande 21185 system, as seen from the surface of a cratered moon

The planet at 16 Cygni B, with a frozen moon

15

The new planets we have found are much bigger than Earth.
Some are as huge as Jupiter and Saturn, the largest planets in
our solar system. Others are even larger than Jupiter.

One of the largest planets we know of is called HD 168443 c.
It is 17 times the mass of Jupiter.

Earth

Jupiter

HD 168443 c

This picture shows the relative masses
of Earth, Jupiter, and HD 168443 c.

There may be smaller planets out there. We just haven't found them yet.
Scientists have a harder time detecting planets the size of Earth from
so far away.

Jupiter and the other large planets in our solar system are giant balls of gas. Many scientists think that the huge extrasolar planets are also made of gas. If you visited one, there might not be a surface to land on.

Someday we may explore extrasolar gas giants. In this picture, a space colony is shown in the distance, through the cloud layers of a gaseous planet.

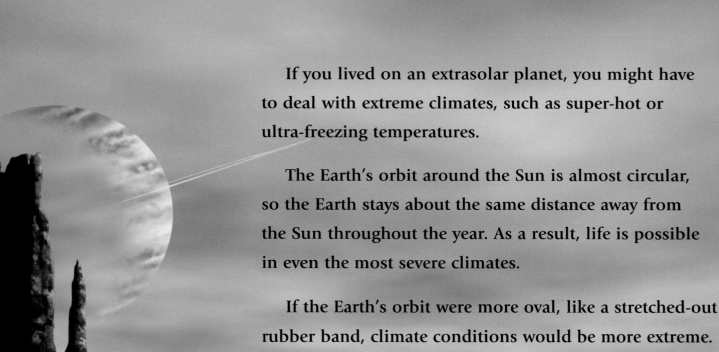

If you lived on an extrasolar planet, you might have to deal with extreme climates, such as super-hot or ultra-freezing temperatures.

The Earth's orbit around the Sun is almost circular, so the Earth stays about the same distance away from the Sun throughout the year. As a result, life is possible in even the most severe climates.

If the Earth's orbit were more oval, like a stretched-out rubber band, climate conditions would be more extreme. When we were closest to the Sun, the oceans might boil from the scalding heat. When we were farthest away, the oceans might freeze from the bitter cold.

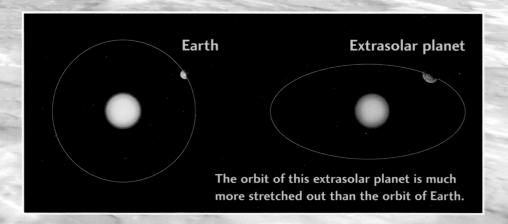

Earth

Extrasolar planet

The orbit of this extrasolar planet is much more stretched out than the orbit of Earth.

Many of the recently discovered planets have stretched-out, oval orbits that produce extreme changes in temperature. These planets bake in the heat, then freeze in the cold, then bake again as they orbit their suns.

Other planets circle so close around their suns that they are red-hot all year round. If you tried to fry an egg on such a planet, the egg would evaporate away in an instant!

The picture on the left shows a planet in an oval orbit when it is so far from its sun that its oceans are frozen. The picture on the right shows the same planet when it is so close to its sun that its oceans boil.

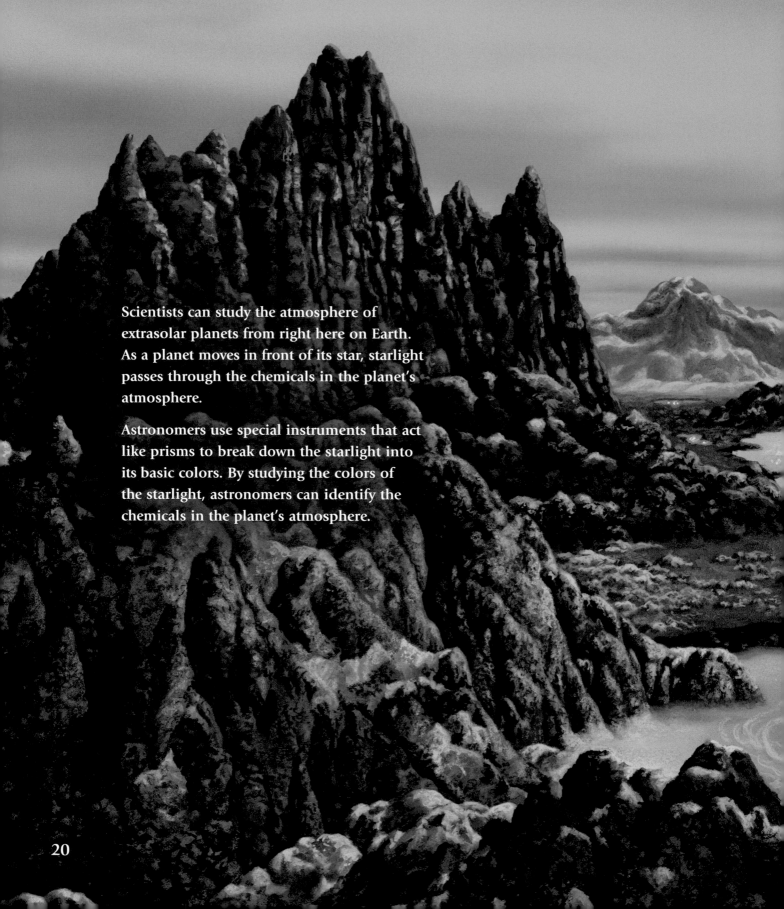

Take a deep breath. Doesn't that fresh, oxygen-rich air feel good?
Breathing would be a lot harder on the extrasolar planets we know about.

Scientists can study the atmosphere of
extrasolar planets from right here on Earth.
As a planet moves in front of its star, starlight
passes through the chemicals in the planet's
atmosphere.

Astronomers use special instruments that act
like prisms to break down the starlight into
its basic colors. By studying the colors of
the starlight, astronomers can identify the
chemicals in the planet's atmosphere.

20

If the newfound planets are like the giant planets in our own solar system, they may have little or no oxygen in their atmospheres. Instead, their air may be thick with poisonous chemicals such as ammonia, methane, and hydrogen sulfide.

Ammonia smells like household cleaning fluids. Methane smells like cow manure. Hydrogen sulfide reeks like rotten eggs. What a foul combination of gases!

A planet with a blue-green sky might have poisonous ammonia, methane, and hydrogen sulfide in the air.

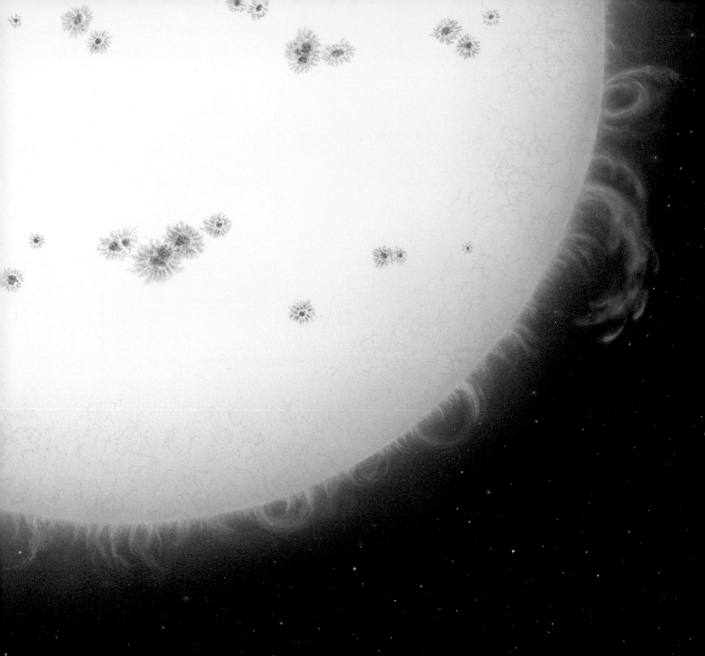

What would it be like to live on an extrasolar planet?

The planet that scientists know the most about is called HD 209458 b. To save our breath, and to conserve precious oxygen, let's call it HD 2-b for short.

HD 2-b orbits a yellow star about 150 light-years away from us. The planet is about 200 times the mass of Earth.

On HD 2-b, a year lasts only 84 hours, or three and a half Earth days. That's how long it takes the planet to travel around its sun. If you lived there, you would have two birthdays every week, and you would be about 100 times your current Earth age!

The outer atmosphere
of HD 2-b is made of hydrogen.
This light gas is slowly leaking out
into space, forming a tail like a comet.
Because of this evaporation, scientists think
that the planet may gradually shrink over time.

HD 2-b orbits close to its sun. This makes the planet extremely hot. Its temperature is estimated to be about 2,000 degrees Fahrenheit, hot enough to melt a copper cooking pot.

The inner atmosphere of the planet contains dangerous sodium gas. Sodium gas explodes when it comes into contact with water and burns when it touches the skin.

**Artist's representation of a research station suspended high above the sodium clouds of planet HD 2-b**

Life on HD 2-b would be a constant struggle. You might live in a self-contained colony ship suspended high above the poisonous, yellow clouds. Special screens would protect you from the intense light of the nearby sun. Super-powerful air conditioners would work continuously to keep the ship cool. In such a hostile environment, there would be no room for errors.

But there would be one good thing about being the first person on HD 2-b: you could give it a new name! You could name it after your pet, or after your favorite food. Would you name it after yourself?

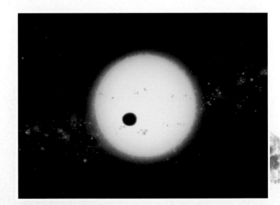

Once every orbit, the planet HD 2-b passes between its star and Earth. Each time this happens, the planet blocks some of the light from the star, and the starlight becomes slightly dimmer. These "shadows" are direct evidence that the planet exists.

No one knows if life exists on HD 2-b or any of the other known extrasolar planets. If it does, the life-forms would not resemble the animals and plants that live on the surface of Earth. The alien life-forms would be well adapted to extreme conditions, such as burning heat, freezing cold, and high pressure. They might thrive on a diet of chemicals, like the tiny organisms that dwell deep within the dark crevices of our planet.

These hypothetical alien life-forms were inspired by actual Earth creatures that cluster around hot thermal vents deep under the sea. The Earth life-forms have adapted to survive intense pressure and no sunshine.

Scientists hope to discover Earth-like planets, with breathable air, drinkable water, and moderate temperatures. Centuries from now, we may be able to travel to these planets and possibly even live there.

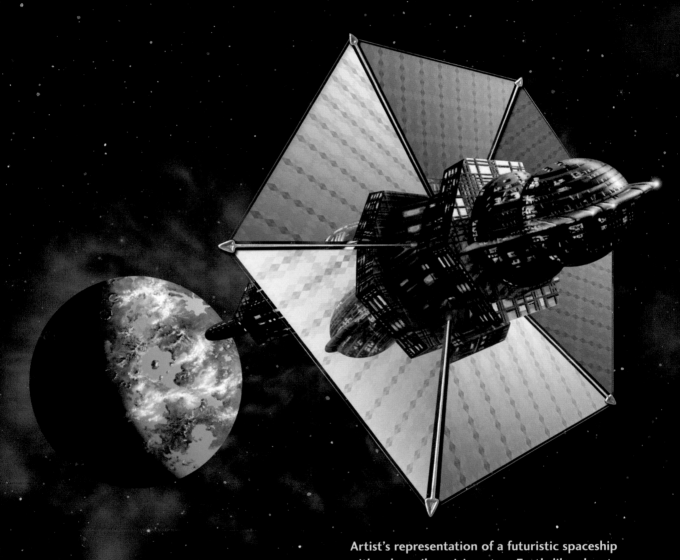

Artist's representation of a futuristic spaceship with solar sails arriving at an Earth-like planet

Scientists are planning a number of missions to search for Earth-like planets. NASA's Kepler spacecraft will carry a special telescope designed to look for the "shadows" of Earth-sized planets as they pass between their suns and Earth. The Darwin project in Europe is developing ways to search for Earth-like planets by sight.

By finding distant worlds, planet hunters pave the way for future exploration. The more planets we find, the more places we can look for alien life. The more living worlds we discover, the more opportunities we will have to contact new civilizations and to find new places to live.

Someday astronauts will journey to planets circling distant stars. They will stand on the shores of alien oceans and marvel at strange new landscapes. They will gaze up at suns once seen only through telescopes.

Maybe you will discover a new planet someday. Maybe you will even get to name it.

And maybe, just maybe, you will lead the quest to discover and explore faraway worlds.

An alien shore on a world with two suns

29

# Some of the Planets in This Book

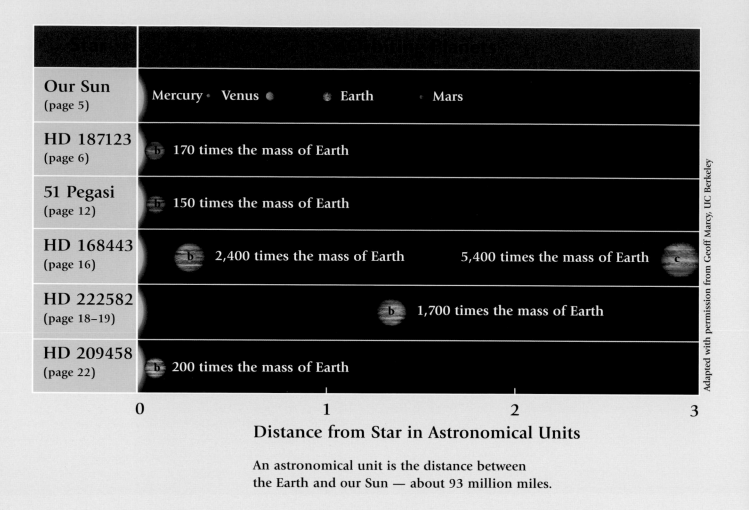

| Star | Some Size and Mass Facts About Orbiting Planets | | |
|------|------|------|------|
| **Our Sun** (page 5) | Mercury · Venus ● · Earth · Mars | | |
| **HD 187123** (page 6) | b 170 times the mass of Earth | | |
| **51 Pegasi** (page 12) | b 150 times the mass of Earth | | |
| **HD 168443** (page 16) | b 2,400 times the mass of Earth | 5,400 times the mass of Earth c | |
| **HD 222582** (page 18–19) | b 1,700 times the mass of Earth | | |
| **HD 209458** (page 22) | b 200 times the mass of Earth | | |

0    1    2    3

### Distance from Star in Astronomical Units

An astronomical unit is the distance between
the Earth and our Sun — about 93 million miles.

Adapted with permission from Geoff Marcy, UC Berkeley

51 Pegasi b, HD 168443 c, HD 209458 b — these planet names sound like license plate numbers! How on Earth did astronomers come up with such names?

Extrasolar planets are named after the stars they orbit. Stars get their names in different ways. Stars like Rigel or Sirius have traditional names, chosen long ago. Some stars, such as 51 Pegasi, are named after the constellation they are in. Other stars take their names from the catalogs in which they were first listed. The stars HD 168443 and HD 209458 were first listed in the Henry Draper Catalog, or HD for short. These stars are the 168,443rd and 209,458th objects listed in the catalog.

When a planet is discovered around a star, it gets the star's name plus a small letter *b*. If other planets are discovered later, they get the letters *c*, *d*, and so on.

# From Science to Art — Painting Faraway Worlds

No one knows what extrasolar planets really look like. We have never visited an extrasolar planet or even taken a direct photograph of one. How does an illustrator paint a planet that no one has ever seen?

In 2000, the California and Carnegie Planet Search team discovered a second planet orbiting the star HD 168443. Artist Lynette R. Cook consulted with team member Geoff Marcy to paint this planet so that others could see what it might look like.

Lynette asked Geoff what was special about the planet. He said that it was so massive that it could be either a planet or a dim, failed star called a brown dwarf. He suggested two paintings showing different possibilities for the planet and the moons that could exist near it.

Back in the studio, Lynette created one illustration showing this world as a ringed planet from the viewpoint of a barren moon. She gave the planet red, orange, and white stripes because it could have many of the same gases as Jupiter. The planet has a bright flare to show that it could be a failed star.

Lynette created a second painting showing the planet and a system of possible moons, as seen from the surface of a moon with liquid water and ice. The sky is blue because the moon has an Earth-like atmosphere. These illustrations have allowed millions of people to imagine a faraway world.

# Glossary

**Astronomer:** A scientist who studies outer space, *4*

**Constellation:** A group of stars that seems to form a pattern, *12*

**Doppler effect:** The way light changes in color or sound changes in pitch when it is given off by an object moving toward or away from an observer, *10*

**Extrasolar planet:** A planet orbiting a star other than our Sun, *4*

**Gravity:** The force that attracts two objects to each other, with a strength that depends on how massive they are, *8*

**Light-year:** The distance light travels in one year — about six trillion miles, *4*

**Mass:** The amount of matter an object contains, *16*

**Orbit:** To travel around an object in a closed, repeating path; also the path itself, *8*

**Planet:** A non-shining object, generally shaped like a ball, that orbits a star, *3*

**Pressure:** How hard something pushes against something else, *26*

**Pulsar:** The rapidly spinning core of a dead star, *13*

**Solar system:** A sun and the bodies that orbit it, including planets, moons, and other objects, *3*

**Visible light:** Light that can be seen by the human eye, *6*

**Wobble method:** A way of discovering planets by measuring their tugs on the stars they orbit, *8*

# Index

# Web Sites